ANCIENT MESOPOTAMIAN GOVERNMENT AND GEOGRAPHY

LAURA LA BELLA

ROSEN
PUBLISHING®

New York

Published in 2017 by The Rosen Publishing Group, Inc.
29 East 21st Street, New York, NY 10010

Copyright © 2017 by The Rosen Publishing Group, Inc.

First Edition

Library of Congress Cataloging-in-Publication Data

Names: La Bella, Laura, author.
Title: Ancient Mesopotamian government and geography / Laura La Bella.
Description: First edition. | New York : Rosen Publishing, 2017. | Series:
  Spotlight on the rise and fall of ancient civilizations | Includes bibliographical
  references and index. | Audience: Grades 7–12.
Identifiers: LCCN 2016003849| ISBN 9781477789100 (library bound) | ISBN
  9781477789094 (pbk.) | ISBN 9781499464207 (6-pack)
Subjects: LCSH: Iraq--Politics and government. | Iraq—History—To 634. |
  Geography, Ancient. | Iraq—Geography.
Classification: LCC DS71 .L23 2016 | DDC 935—dc23
LC record available at http://lccn.loc.gov/2016003849

Manufactured in the United States of America

CONTENTS

GEOGRAPHY AND GOVERNMENT: SHAPING A CIVILIZATION

Mesopotamia, a Greek word meaning "land between the rivers," was an ancient region of southwestern Asia. It encompassed what is now Iraq, plus parts of modern-day Syria and Turkey. This is where the world's earliest civilizations developed. Mesopotamia is known as one of the cradles of civilization.

Two significant developments occurred in Mesopotamia. The region was bounded by two major rivers that made the land fertile for farming; this rich soil encouraged people to settle into permanent communities. The result was the rise of cities—an urban center that contained numerous buildings surrounded by a dense population of people.

The second major development was the invention of writing and written language. Spurred by the rise of cities, the Sumerians invented writing as a way to communicate their needs during trade. As needs grew and trade expanded, a written form of communication became necessary. Writing became the way people communicated across great distances and between the growing cities in Mesopotamia.

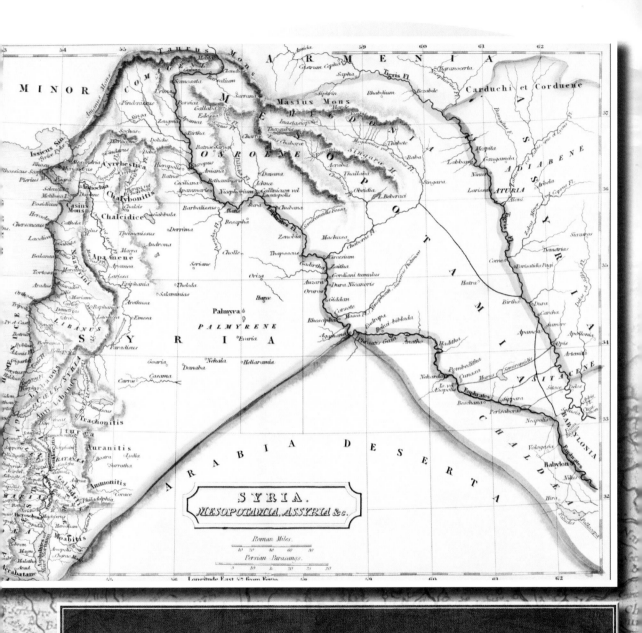

This map of Mesopotamia shows where in relation the region sits, as well as its proximity to the Tigris and Euphrates River systems.

WHAT IS A CIVILIZATION?

A civilization is an advanced state of human society. In a civilization, there is a high level of culture, science, industry, and government. A clearly defined geographic area and a functioning government define a civilization.

The fertile soil in Mesopotamia meant people could grow food. As a result, people settled together and began growing food and domesticating animals for use as a community. As larger groups of people settled together, they needed a set of rules to guide life in these communities. The need for a system of government grew.

When people live together as a community, a system of rules keeps order and guides societal life. That system of rules, called a government, provides guidance on how people will live and behave together, how trade will be conducted, which jobs people will hold to keep the community running smoothly, and who will serve as a leader for the group as a whole.

This stone tablet, or relief, titled "Relief from Royal Palaces of Nineveh," was one of thousands recovered from seventh-century Assyrian civilization. Stone tablets were carved with scenes from everyday life.

WHERE WAS MESOPOTAMIA?

Mesopotamia included the land between the Euphrates and Tigris Rivers, in a section of the present-day region known as the Middle East. Mesopotamia was roughly 300 miles (482 kilometers) long and 150 miles (241 km) wide. Mesopotamia boarded the Zagros Mountains in the northeast and the Arabian Plateau in the southeast.

Mesopotamia was first settled by the Sumerians around 3500 BCE. Prior to this time, most people lived on farms in the country and fended for themselves. The area had few roads, so the Tigris and Euphrates Rivers were critical to daily life. The rivers provided water for farming, bathing, drinking, and cleaning, and they served as a means for travel and trade. Boats carrying various goods traveled on river currents to and from different cities to conduct trade.

As more and more people settled in the area, cities such as Ur, Uruk, Lagash, and Kish were built in Sumer, an ancient civilization and a historical region in Mesopotamia. They were called city-states.

The Zagros Mountains, which are located in modern-day Iran, were the northeast border of Mesopotamia.

TWO MAJOR CONTRIBUTIONS

Mesopotamia is credited with two significant contributions to the world: the rise of the city and the invention of writing.

The world's first cities began to appear in Mesopotamia between 4000 and 3500 BCE. The increase in a concentrated population led to the establishment of cities. City life allowed people to work together for the common good.

The following factors distinguish a city from a settlement:

- Significant population
- Buildings
- Some form of sewer/sanitation system
- Basic governmental structure
- Walls and/or fortifications for protection
- Defined geographical area

The Sumerians invented writing as a means of communication for trade between cities. The earliest form of writing was pictographs—symbols that represented objects—and aided traders in remembering which goods went to each destination.

This relief depicts some major contributions from Mesopotamia, including the wheel, walled structures, and buildings.

OF NORTH AND SOUTH

Mesopotamia was made up of Northern (or Upper) Mesopotamia and Southern (or Lower) Mesopotamia. Each had distinct geography and natural resources.

In Northern Mesopotamia's hills and plains, seasonal rains, rivers, and streams created fertile land. Settlers farmed the land and used its natural resources, including forest timber, metals from the earth, and stone, to build houses and farms. Their government primarily guided the rules and laws around farming and crop distribution.

Southern Mesopotamia consisted of marshy areas and plains. Cities developed along the region's rivers. Early settlers irrigated land along the rivers so their crops could grow. Their government created rules and guidance to help large populations live together as a society.

Because neither region had many natural resources, trade with neighboring lands was required. Southern Mesopotamian life centered around trade on the Euphrates and Tigris Rivers. Trade was difficult for Northern Mesopotamians, because few roads existed to move goods.

A cylinder seal is a small stone tube with a scene, like this marsh hunt, carved into its surface and rolled on wet clay to make a copy of the image.

THE FERTILE CRESCENT: NUTRIENT SOIL FOR GOOD FARMING

The Euphrates and Tigris Rivers were vital for agricultural development in Mesopotamia. As the rains and melting mountain snow drained onto the plains, nutrient-rich soil called silt was deposited onto the plains. This made the soil fertile, making it easy for farmers to grow crops. The Fertile Crescent, the common name for this area because of its crescent shape, includes all of Mesopotamia as well as the land around the Nile River in Egypt.

Farmers grew a wide range of crops, including barley and wheat, peas, beans and lentils, cucumbers, leeks (part of the onion family), lettuces, garlic, grapes, apples, melons, and figs. Combined with livestock such as goats, poultry, and sheep, people had a diet rich in fruits and vegetables, butter, milk, and meat.

Sheep and goats were also important for their wool and hair. These animals were sheared, or shaved, and their wool and hair were used to make clothing and blankets.

Caspian
Sea

Tigris River

Mediterranean
Sea

C r e s c e n t

Euphrates River

F e r t i l e

Nile River

Red Sea

Persian Gulf

N
W   E
S

© 2012 Encyclopædia Britannica, Inc

The Tigris and Euphrates Rivers cut through the Fertile Crescent, making the soil of the region nutritious for plants and crops.

LIFE ALONG THE RIVERS

People settled along the Euphrates and Tigris Rivers to be close to the waterways for trade and travel and to use the fertile soil fed by the rivers. As government emerged, so did the maintenance of farming and crop distribution. Local governments worked to manage farming so the community could better withstand a famine or drought that might otherwise affect crop production.

The agricultural season started in late October and early November, when land was prepared for planting. If the rainy season was delayed, then crops did not grow and famine followed. To mediate the impact of a famine, the government regulated farming so food was available year round. Harvesting occurred from the end of April until June.

There was very little annual rainfall; farmers relied mostly on snow runoff from the mountains and water from the rivers. There were seasons of cooler weather and seasons of very hot weather.

The Euphrates River was crucial to life in Mesopotamia and still is. For example, hydropower stations and modern irrigation pipelines have been constructed to transport water over long distances.

LIVING IN THE DESERT

Mesopotamia was mostly desert, and living there was extremely hard. It was brutally hot with temperatures rising to 110 degrees Fahrenheit (43 degrees Celsius) or more in the summer months. There was also little to no shade from forests or trees. Mesopotamia's limited forests also meant there was little wood available that could be used for building. The region had few options for practical building materials, so people had to use what they could. Mud was used to create bricks and to make plaster. It was far from ideal; the mud would crumble in the hot, dry environment.

The region also had few mountains or natural barriers, such as coasts, waterways, or rocky cliffs, to help keep invaders away. The region was invaded on a regular basis. People often stole from one another. Some city-states attempted to unify the entire region by conquering all of the other city-states to create one large territory.

This brick is what was used in Mesopotamia to build houses and other structures. The bricks were fired, or dried under intensive heat, to make them harder and stronger.

THE ANCIENT CANAL SYSTEM

An elaborate canal system for irrigation linked the major cities of Mesopotamia. This was a major factor in the civilization and modernization of Mesopotamia. Irrigation, a process used to bring water to areas that have too little, was invented in Mesopotamia. In order to move water through the desert, the people of Mesopotamia built a large, connected network of canals that linked various city-states.

The canal system provided water for farming and for sanitation in the city-states. This system redirected water from the Euphrates and Tigris Rivers to farming land so crops could be watered on a regular basis. Some canals also flowed into cities for sanitation and for use by the general population for bathing, washing, and cooking.

The canal system also protected Mesopotamia from flooding. Using a system of gated ditches and levees, people could control the flow of water to avoid flooding during heavy rainfall or when winter snows in the mountains melted too quickly. They also controlled the water to maintain crops and facilitate crop growth.

This stone relief shows how an aqueduct brings water from the rivers using irrigation channels. This method of transporting water enabled farming to thrive in the region.

GOVERNMENT

Kings ruled Mesopotamia. However, the kings only ruled over one city-state, not an entire kingdom or region. Each king decided the rules for their city-state that they thought would be most beneficial for their people.

The central governmental building in each city-state was the ziggurat. A ziggurat is a type of pyramid with stepped sides and a flat top. The ziggurat was part of a temple complex that included courtyards, storage rooms, bathing rooms, and living areas. Each ziggurat was the center for business, religion, and government. Kings and priests gathered here to make laws and rules, and to oversee society.

The government established the functions for each group of people in society and determined how things were to be done. The government decided what would be taxed, how to collect the taxes, and which public projects (for example, digging irrigation systems or expanding the size of cities) would be undertaken. They also set farming quotas to establish a consistent, steady food supply.

The Ur of the Chaldees was a historic ziggurat that is still in existence today. Its location is in Southern Iraq.

RELIGION, CULTURE, AND THE CITY-STATES

While religion differed slightly between each city-state, all of Mesopotamia's city-states were polytheistic. Each city-state centered around one main god or goddess believed to watch over the city and its population. They also believed kings descended from gods.

Mesopotamians worshipped hundreds of gods and goddesses and offered up gifts and sacrifices to keep them happy. If something bad happened, such as a flood or other natural disaster, they believed that an unhappy god or goddess had caused the disaster in order to punish the people. Mesopotamians made offerings at the ziggurats to stay on their gods' good side or to regain their favor. People believed they each had a personal god who provided guidance and protection.

Some gods were connected to specific professions. The major gods included:

- Anu: father of the gods and the god of the sky
- Enlil: god of air
- Utu: sun god and the lord of truth and justice

The goddess Astarte, as shown on a terracotta relief. Gods and goddesses were revered in ancient Mesopotamia. Astarte was the Goddess of Fertility, Beauty, War, and Love.

- Nanna: moon god
- Inanna: goddess of love and war
- Ninhursag: goddess of earth
- Enki: god of fresh water and lord of wisdom and magic

City-states were centers of trade and business, as well as the epicenter for learning and cultural diffusion, or the spreading of culture, art, education and religion. This was important because it helped each region advance together instead of keeping everyone isolated. When ideas are shared, new ideas grow. As people traveled between different city-states for trade, they shared ideas about religion, art, education, and even food. This infusion of ideas and culture helped each community grow and adopt new ways of doing things. Governments learned how other city-states operated and made adjustments to laws and rules to improve life for its people. Trade also brought in money, which brought in intellectuals who invented new tools or ways of doing things.

Mesopotamians also celebrated their culture through festivals, ceremonies, and traditions. There were rituals and ceremonies for various rites of passage, such as birth, death, and marriage.

During sacrificial ceremonies, people made offerings to a god and goddess in hopes of protection, rain during times of drought, or help in other aspects of their everyday life.

AKKADIAN EMPIRE

Four empires ruled Mesopotamia: the Akkadian, Babylonian, Assyrian, and Neo-Babylonian. All governed differently, and each made contributions to today's way of life.

The Akkadian Empire was the first empire of Mesopotamia and first in the entire world. Their greatest king, Sargon of Akkad, established the concept of an empire as a way to rule over a large region of land and a diverse population of people.

The most significant result of Akkadian rule was language. The Akkadians introduced their language, also called Akkadian, which became the official language of the empire and the basis for the modern-day languages of Aramaic and Arabic.

The Akkadian Empire united dozens of city-states and created two spheres of influence to recognize the divergent cultures of Northern Mesopotamia and Southern Mesopotamia, which had developed different ways of life because of their geography. Northern Mesopotamia was wet and mountainous; Southern Mesopotamia was flat desert.

This is an Akkadian inscription on a brick-stamp of baked clay. The Akkadians introduced a common language, which became the foundation of several modern-day languages.

BABYLONIAN EMPIRE

The Babylonian Empire gained control of the southern portion of the Akkadian Empire, also known as Southern Mesopotamia. They changed very little of what the Akkadians had established.

The Babylonian Empire is most well known for a code of law create by their greatest king, King Hammurabi. As he conquered more and more city-states, Hammurabi realized he needed a common set of rules to control the diverse groups of people now under his control.

He sent legal experts throughout his kingdom to collect all of the existing laws in the city-states now under his control. He reviewed them all, kept some, and threw out others. He narrowed the list to 282 laws, the most well known of these today is "an eye for an eye, a tooth for a tooth." These laws were put in place not only to punish those who committed crimes, but also to protect the weak from the strong.

This stone relief is a carving of King Hammurabi at worship. His Code of Hammurabi was a well-preserved code of law that governed the way of life in ancient Babylon.

ASSYRIAN EMPIRE

The Assyrian Empire was best known for its military power and conquests. The Assyrian Army was well trained and organized into units of charioteers, cavalry, bowmen, or lancers. Each unit was trained in their given area and became proficient in their specific fighting style.

The Assyrian Army also became ruthless in warfare. They established a corps of engineers who developed moveable towers, iron battering rams, and other dangerous weapons. They built roads to more easily move their army through Mesopotamia in order to attack city-states and areas they wanted to conquer. They also tortured their foes. The Assyrians became the most feared civilization in ancient history.

When the Assyrians conquered a city-state, they forced the conquered people to pay taxes. Taxes led to great wealth for the Assyrian Empire.

The Assyrians also introduced their own dialect of Akkadian. Aramaic, which became the most commonly used language in the region, is still spoken there today.

This relief shows the brutal treatment of prisoners by the Assyrian Army, one of the most ruthless armies in world history.

NEO-BABYLONIAN EMPIRE

The Neo-Babylonian Empire began when the Babylonians took control of Mesopotamia for a second time and established a new empire. Their most famous king was Nebuchadnezzar II, a ruthless military leader.

The Neo-Babylonians became well known for their architecture and for the beauty of the city of Babylon, which Nebuchadnezzar II rebuilt during his rule. Beautiful, decorated walls made from dyed, baked tiles were erected around the city. Nebuchadnezzar II had towers built, where archers stood guard to protect the city, and a moat dug around Babylon. At times of war the moat's bridges were dismantled to ensure the city's safety.

The Babylonians also became known for their skills and discoveries in mathematics and astronomy. They created the first sundial, a device used to tell the time of day by the position of the sun. This led to the development of our present-day system of a sixty-minute hour and a seven-day week.

In the Biblical story "Four in the Flames," King Nebuchadnezzar II threw three men into the fires for refusing to bow, the son of God saves them.

TEMPLES, KINGS, AND GODS

The temple at the center of every city-state symbolized the importance of that city's god. It was believed that the gods were present in the planning and execution of all public works projects. People recited specific prayers to certain gods and believed that these acts were vitally important for the success of a new construction venture.

Mesopotamians believed their kings were descended from gods, but they never viewed their kings as gods or as powerful as gods. However, each city-state's king, who set the laws and oversaw the government, was considered powerful enough to represent the gods and their will through his own commands. A king dealt directly with the people and viewed their feedback on his decisions as vital. Many kings changed laws or other aspects of their governmental structure if the people demanded it.

Prior to kings, priests ruled the city-states and were believed to dictate laws from divine messages sent by the gods.

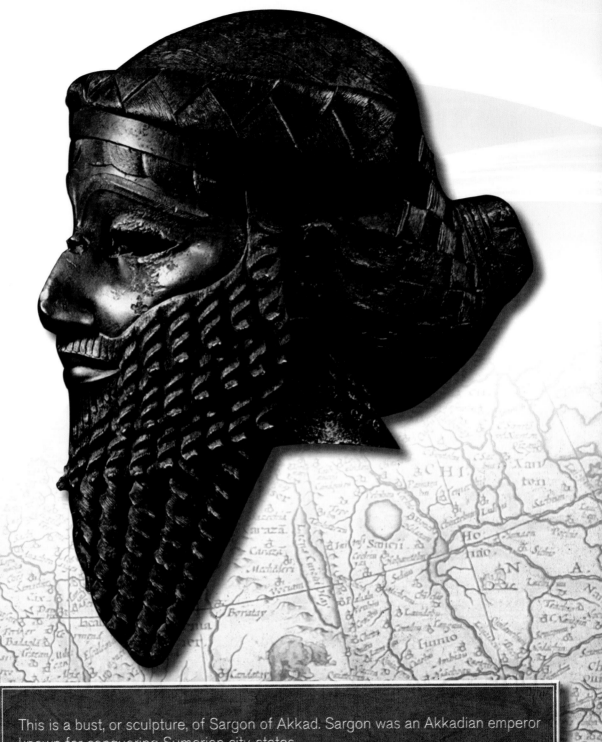

This is a bust, or sculpture, of Sargon of Akkad. Sargon was an Akkadian emperor known for conquering Sumerian city-states.

WARFARE: THE STRUGGLE FOR POWER

Warfare originated in Mesopotamia. History's first recorded war was between Sumer and Elam in 2700 BCE. The first use of the bow and arrow as a weapon can also be traced to Mesopotamia.

As city-states began to grow in population, their geographic regions overlapped other city-states and disagreements ensued about politics, religion, or land. Warfare became part of the Mesopotamian culture as one city-state engaged in war with another. It was common for a neutral city-state to mediate or assist in an argument between two other regions. This sort of cooperation lead to unions and alliances between city-states, eventually leading to larger, regional states.

After empires began conquering various city-states, war expanded to foreign countries and the geography and boarders of Mesopotamia constantly changed. As a sign of their strength, size, and influence, many palace walls in the Assyrian and Babylonian Empires were decorated with pictures of battles fought and won by each empire.

The Mesopotamian region was a center for warfare for hundreds of years as empires rose and fell. The use of chariots in war dates back to Sumerians in 2400 BCE.

THE HISTORICAL INFLUENCE OF MESOPOTAMIA

So many developments (writing and language), modern-day inventions (the wheel, the sundial, and weaponry), and scientific discoveries (astronomy and mathematics) can be traced back to Mesopotamia, the world's first civilization. A collection of cultures defined this civilization as they fed, influenced, and grew together. It was an epicenter for education and learning, for agricultural development, and for religious enlightenment. Trade and commerce across this geographically diverse region led to an infusion of cultures, where distinct societies that were once separated by geography meshed together and became part of a shared Mesopotamian culture.

Mesopotamia was also among the first societies to use a structured governmental system to unify the various people and cultures that spread across its vast, distinct geography. As people settled in Mesopotamia and city-states grew in population, the world's first rules and laws were established to help guide life in these communities. Government became vital to the way of life and provided a structure for behavior and conducting business.

This Phoenician ivory dagger handle in the form of a lion is an example of the numerous cultural and scientific developments that date back to Mesopotamia.

GLOSSARY

agriculture The practice of farming the land and growing crops for food and raising animals as livestock for food and other resources.

astronomy The study of objects in space.

battering ram A heavy weapon that is struck against a door to demolish it.

bowmen Warriors who use bows and arrows in battle.

cavalry A group of soldiers trained to fight on horseback.

charioteer A warrior who drives a chariot during battle.

corps A military group with a specialized function.

deity Another word for god.

demarcation Setting geographic boundaries.

descended To be related to an individual from a previous generation.

ditch A narrow trench or passageway for water to travel.

enlightenment A state of high awareness.

famine A severe shortage of food.

fortification To strengthen or make stronger.

harvest To gather crops when they become ripe or fully grown.

irrigation To supply water to an area via canals and waterways.

lancer A warrior armed with a lance, or a spearlike weapon.

levee An embankment near a river or waterway that is raised to prevent flooding.

plowing To break up and prepare soil for growing crops.

polytheistic The belief in more than one god.

quota An allotment assigned to a person or group that needs to be met.

sanitation Relating to conditions of the public's health, such as clean water to drink.

FOR MORE INFORMATION

Association of Ancient Historians
Western Illinois University
1 University Cir.
Morgan Hall 438
Macomb, IL 61455-1390
Website: associationofancienthistorians.org
The Association of Ancient Historians (AAH) fosters thought and
    discussion on ancient history. The organization is open to anyone
    interested in ancient history or specific periods of ancient history.

The Canadian Society for Mesopotamian Studies
c/o RIM Project
University of Toronto
4 Bancroft Avenue, 4th floor
Toronto, Ontario
Canada
M5S 1C1
(416) 978-4531
Email: csms@chass.utoronto.ca
Website: http://projects.chass.utoronto.ca/csms/main.html
Founded in 1980, The Canadian Society for Mesopotamian Studies
examines the literature, culture, and history of ancient Mesopotamia.

The Historical Association
59a Kennington Park Road
London SE11 4JH
England
Website: www.history.org.uk
A teacher training and development site, The Historical Association
    focuses on various areas of history, including ancient history and
    ancient civilizations.

Society for Classical Studies
University of Pennsylvania
220 S. 40th Street
Suite 201E
Philadelphia, PA 19104-3512
(215) 898-4975
Website: https://classicalstudies.org
The Society for Classical Studies is the primary society for the study and understanding of ancient languages, literatures, and civilizations.

The World History Association (WHA)
Meserve Hall
Northeastern University
360 Huntington Avenue
Boston, MA 02115 USA
(617) 373-6818
Website: www.thewha.org
The World History Association (WHA) promotes the teaching and research of world history. It specializes in many areas of study and scholarship, including ancient history and the origins of the Middle East.

WEBSITES

Because of the changing nature of Internet links, Rosen Publishing has developed an online list of websites related to the subject of this book. This site is updated regularly. Please use this link to access the list:

http://www.rosenlinks.com/SRFAC/mgov

FOR FURTHER READING

Apte, Sunita. *Mesopotamia*. New York, NY: Children's Press, 2010.

Blattner, Don. *World Civilizations and Cultures*. Greensboro, NC: Mark Twain Media/Carson-Dellosa Publishing Group, 2012.

Burbank, Jane, and Fredrick Cooper. *Empires in World History: Power and the Politics of Difference*. Princeton, NJ: Princeton University Press, 2011.

Cline, Eric H., and Mark W. Graham. *Ancient Empires: From Mesopotamia to the Rise of Islam*. New York, NY: Cambridge University Press, 2011.

James, Simon. *Ancient Rome*. New York, NY: DK Children, 2015.

Kriwaczek, Paul. *Babylon: Mesopotamia and the Birth of Civilization*. New York, NY: St. Martin's Griffin Press, 2012.

Lassieur, Allison. *The Ancient World: Ancient Mesopotamia*. New York, NY: Children's Press, 2012.

Miller, Gary G. *The Tigris and Euphrates: Rivers of the Fertile Crescent*. New York, NY: Crabtree Publishing Company, 2010.

Pearson, Anne. *Ancient Greece*. New York, NY: DK Children, 2014.

Woods, Michael. *Ancient Agricultural Technology: From Sickles to Plows*. Minneapolis, MN: Twenty-First Century Books/Lerner Publishing Group, 2011.

BIBLIOGRAPHY

"The Akkadian Period (ca. 2350-2150 B.C.)." The Metropolitan Museum of Art. 2016. Retrieved January 5, 2016 (http://www.metmuseum.org/toah/hd/akka/hd_akka.htm).

"Ancient Iraq (Mesopotamia)." Ancient Civilization for Kids. Retrieved January 6, 2016 (https://sites.google.com/site/1ancientcivilizationsforkids/ancient-iraq-mesopotamia).

"Ancient Mesopotamian Facts." Kids Connect. Retrieved January 5, 2016 (https://kidskonnect.com/history/ancient-mesopotamia/).

"Assyrians: Cavalry and Conquests." The Independence Hall Association. 2014. Retrieved January 7, 2016 (http://www.ushistory.org/civ/4d.asp).

"The Fertile Crescent." Retrieved January 7, 2016 (http://www.kidspast.com/world-history/0035b-fertile-cresent.php).

"The Four Empires of Mesopotamia." Study.com. 2016. Retrieved January 6, 2016 (http://study.com/academy/lesson/the-four-empires-of-mesopotamia.html).

Mark, Joshua J. "The Ancient City." Ancient History Encyclopedia. April 5, 2014. Retrieved January 4, 2016 (http://www.ancient.eu/city/).

Mark, Joshua J. "Mesopotamia." Ancient History Encyclopedia. September 2, 2009. Retrieved January 4, 2016 (http://www.ancient.eu/Mesopotamia/)

Mark, Joshua J. "Nebuchadnezzar II." Ancient History Encyclopedia. July 20, 2010. Retrieved January 5, 2016 (http://www.ancient.eu/Nebuchadnezzar_II/).

Mark, Joshua J. "Writing." Ancient History Encyclopedia. April 28, 2011. Retrieved January 5, 2016 (http://www.ancient.eu/writing/).

"Mesopotamia: Geography." The British Museum. Retrieved January 4, 2016 (http://www.mesopotamia.co.uk/geography/home_set.html).

"The Rise of Sumerian City-States." Teacher's Curriculum Institute. 2010. Retrieved January 6, 2016 (http://www.teachtci.com/programs/middle-school/history-alive-textbook/ancient-world/MS-History-Alive-The-Ancient-World-Textbook-Sample-Chapter.pdf).

INDEX

ABOUT THE AUTHOR

Laura La Bella is a writer and the author of more than 30 nonfiction children's books. She has written several historical books covering events or periods of history, including the Holocaust and the Songhay Empire. La Bella lives in Rochester, New York, with her husband and sons.

PHOTO CREDITS